Musings of a Moonchild

Gayatri Batchu

BookLeaf Publishing

India | USA | UK

Presentation by *BookLeaf Publishing*

Web: www.bookleafpub.com

E-mail: info@bookleafpub.com

ISBN: 9789360941444

First edition 2024

I want to express my gratitude to my Father and Mother for being my unwavering pillars of strength. My sister and brother, thank you for being my best friends and always having my back. To my friends who always stood by me through the highs and lows. Without your support, this book would not have come to fruition. Without you, I cannot imagine who I would be today, nor would this book have come to life. Thank you all.

Moon

Stars shine
The dark night,
My heart calls
For a bright light.

A darkness swirls in my heart,
The kind others can never know.
Only when the full moon rises,
Does hope find its way once again.

Salvation

Frozen time
Healing scars
A broken heart
Runs a mindless rut.

Flowers sent
To make amends
Forgiveness sought
After a fatal wound.

Deep inside
A voice whispers,
Never return to him,
Who is unsure of thee.

Holding on is never the answer
For him who doesn't deserve.
Goodbye is the only salvation
A single way to save myself.

The Evil Eye (Nazar)

Fire meant to cleanse
From eyes that burn dark.
Turning me to ashes,
Leaving me on the cold ground.

Cannot see me shine
Looking for ways to shame.
Jealousy in their veins,
Cursing for my pain.

My mother wields the fire,
meant to lift me back.
Like the very Phoenix
Rising high in the sky.

Chandelier

Born with a white heart that reflects,
The whole world it captures.
Pure and white,
No distortions exist.

While we are born completely
Life happens.
Cracking the beautiful shape
Which each of us has been uniquely gifted.

Broken pieces adorn the path
Each one of us takes.
No single alike,
In darkness astray.

On a blue moon night when the question arises
How to feel complete again?
Then the quest to make the chandelier begins.
Anew to the one we started with.

Getting to be creators of our hearts now.
Finding happiness along the way.
Different light that shines,
To each their own.
Finds its way from deep within.

Generation Gap

Bound by unsaid rules
Made by unknown fools.
Freedom is a crime,
Jail us with expectations.

Clipping our wings,
In the name of happiness.
Bounding us,
In the name of compassion.

Who will tell them?
The world has changed,
No more is it 1960s
For 23 to be the right age.

MBBS Escapade

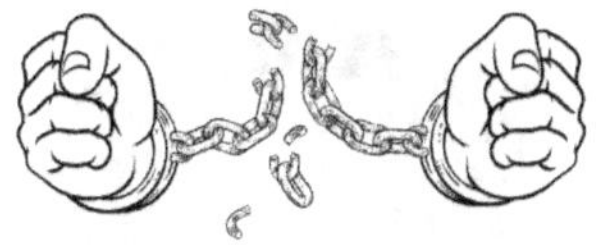

In the mirage of multicolored lights,
I breathe again after a very long time.
Most of the day was filled with wailing cries,
The sound of music soothes my soul.

Loud enough to make the floor shake,
Dancing hard enough to forget every single
name.
It's an escape from my life,
Witnessing death every day.

Saving lives is an honor being granted.
Worked tirelessly to make this happen.
Now that I'm here,
It's a struggle to remember my purpose,
Why I wanted this in the first place.

A whisper-like wind ran my breath,
What is the point of saving others
When I'm unable to save myself?
Yet, for now, I'll forget the darkness that looms
And be the light for someone else tomorrow
again.

Mind

I have been living in my head for a while.
On a loop in memories and imagination,
Became numb to the world around,
The present moment passed away in a blur.

Mind is a wonder.
Magical enough to trap me in or set me free.
And it all comes down to our choice,
It's all about choosing wisely.

Once I remember this fact,
It sets me free.
Once again making me a possibility,
To the spell of life.

Courage

I never really accepted myself
Let others' thoughts weigh me down.
Only when I started to listen to my heart,
Did I finally find the courage,
To chase my dreams.

Maiden's Musing

Uncertain path ahead
A choice already made
Truth that unfolds
Leaving a terrible ache.
Three knots promised to tie
But deep inside a voice asks
Is he the right one?
Questions start pounding,
Will I lose my happiness in the quest to make a
family?
But after the promises are made,
Is there really a way back to my old life again?

The Truth

In the abyss of unknown
Lies the truth.
"Everything that exists today,
Will die when the time arrives."

Living like we are promised tomorrow,
Worrying over simple sorrows.
Awareness of the truth,
To take ourselves less seriously.

So don't hold on too tight,
To your joys or sorrows.
To your laughter or tears.
To friends or foes.

Relax
Take a deep breath
And let life sweep you in its magic.
For the truth of death only sets you free.

Tug of war

Restless energy,
Hoping for a release.
Wanting to break free
From invisible barricades.

Split between,
Wanting to stay or running away.
Familiar land or uncharted territories.
New faces or the same old.

In the end, it is a tug of war between,
Flying away or staying on the ground.
Both have a price to pay,
Only one is the right call.

Lost

Laptop in hand
Doubts in my bag.
Tag in my neck
Getting ready to work.

Working with deadlines,
Same old conversations.
That's when I wonder
What am I doing here?

All my life, I've been told
A job was supposed to be the answer.
Studied hard to be right here.
But now that I'm here,
All I can feel is lost.

Monotonous life goes
Slowly I lost the colour,
Black and white is all I see
If this was supposed to be the answer,
Why do I feel so lost?

Dining Table

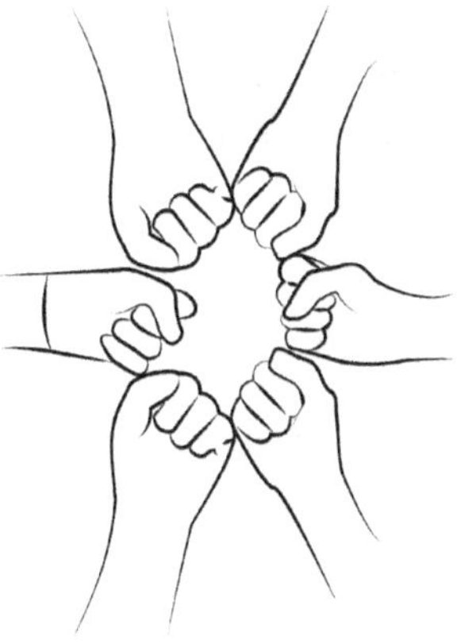

Mother's cooked food in the middle
Never-ending small conversations.
Few taunts, more laughter.
Sharing stories of how the day went for each of
us.

Staying together is a joy like no other.
This time is the one I always look forward to.
My greatest strength and my source of energy.
Love overflows right from this core of mine.

Simple things together,
Makes it better.
It makes my life beautiful.
A wooden dining table like this,
Becomes a source of bliss.

At those moments
Happiness doesn't seem so complicated.
I don't have to do a lot,
To just have a hearty laugh.

Pause

Days like these,
When I don't want to leave my bed.
Binge-watch my favorite shows.
Recharging my tired mind.

Eating my soul food,
Catching up with my friends.
Letting my thoughts rest,
And let my heart be at peace.

Slowing down my pace,
And hitting my breaks.
To take a long breath of air,
A small pause I take.

To refresh myself.
Resetting my perspective.
To look at the world,
Brand new again.

Resilience

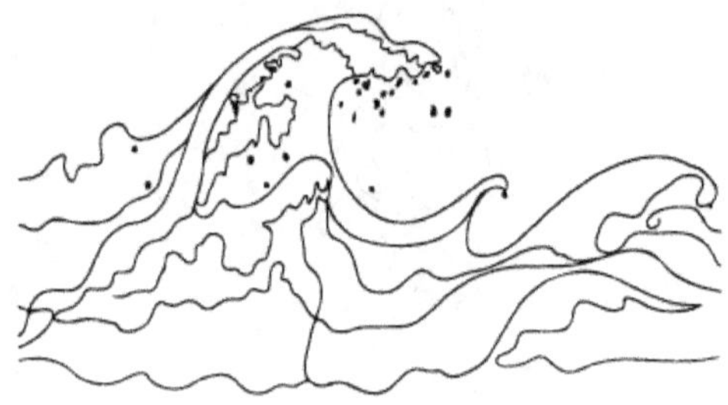

The harder you fall,
The higher you will fly.
But that is only possible,
When you don't get crushed in the process.

It's easier said than done,
To get up after every fall.
When your heart is broken,
Mending it never turns it back to how it was.

A silver ray of hope dawns,
When my passion sparks.
I remember the joy of writing,
And start counting my blessings along the way.

Rising and falling,
Is the way the tide flows.
Accepting the reality,
I let resilience sink into my new identity.

Opposite

Freedom is what we seek,
But forget if we can handle it.
The vastness it holds,
The uncertainty it gives.
Ultimately leaves us to suffer.

We want certainty,
A success in everything.
Grades, job, and love.
Control is our greatest virtue,
Predicting the future is an obsession.

But freedom is wild,
It cannot be tamed into control.
When what we seek
And what we want are opposite,
Can we ever really be free?

Phantoms

The night scares me,
Not for the silence.
But for that which comes alive in the darkness.

Pandora's box in me
Becomes unguarded.
It sees the chance to open up.

Demons from the past creep in,
Shaking up my very being.
Unable to sleep, I lay awake.

Fighting the invisible phantoms
In my head.

Baton

A small word of encouragement
A kind little smile
Makes the day of a weary heart
On the roadside.

Kindness is hard to find
Amid the chaos of the world.
But a simple action has the power
to change the trajectory of a stranger's day.

Everyone of us
Can pass the baton,
At our very own pace.
To make this world a better place.

Guilt trip

When things don't go their way,
Silent treatment is the tool they wield
Age card is brought up—
Elders should be respected.

When things don't go their way,
They emotionally manipulate
To guilt trip you to follow their choice at the
end.

But it is not needed to shoulder the
responsibility
Of fragile egos.
Guilt is induced to control.
Your life is your own to live.
It doesn't have to be on others' whims.

Flashback

Sometimes I tend to go back in time
And find the ones I've left behind.
I turned my back when things got too hard
And never reached the destination I chose to
walk.

And now,
While the ones who were by my side were
hiking peaks.
I tended to my wounds down in the valley.
Piece by piece I healed my broken heart.

While I left the purpose I was flying for.
From the ground, I look at the sky
At the remnants of the past
The trajectory of my next voyage has changed,
As I fly towards a new beginning.

Cold Chills

The idea of marriage,
Brings cold chills down my veins
While everyone is waiting for the day
I don't.

The idea of commitment for life
It makes me scared of the unknown
Letting go of my freedom
It is something I'm afraid of.

I try to voice my thoughts
It gets lost in the winds of chatter.
I try to shield my heart
For being the only anomaly.

Karma

You are the slow poison
A snake shedding its skin
The world thinks you are noble
Behind the doors you let the mask fall.

Expert in the art of manipulation.
Turning everyone against your target.
After the war is fought.
Of course, nothing is your fault.

Conveniently you shift the blame.
An effort to keep your conscience clean.
But remember,
You can never escape karma.

Hyenas

Toxicity running in their veins
Cannot be happy for others' joy
Blood is the chain that bounds
Made of steel that doesn't rust.

Enemies are not strangers
But from people within
Brooding envious eyes
Hyenas preying on mistakes.

Gaslighting and insulting
Pushing a person to the corner in disdain
Loneliness is what one feels.
One wrong word would inflame fragile egos.
For the sake of retaining an image of family.
One bears the brunt of toxicity while praying not
to lose one's self.

War

I have been sinking in sorrow
Running in my head
Losing track of time and place.
The war in my head
Never ceases to die.
Bleeding invisible to the world
Ammunition running out
Demons outnumbered
In the dark of night, left alone.
Hoping for the sun to come out.
Surging ahead to survive
Not wanting to give up.
"You either fall or rise,"
And my choice has been made
When I stood on my shaky feet.

Guru

Your unbounded grace
For the one who gets lost all too many times
Is boundless.

You patiently wait
For the youngling to grow
Through all the tantrums
You never stop having faith

Spinning in circles
Crying over the loop of suffering
And when it gets too hard
You show the way forward again.

Magic is your way of being
Guiding me in more ways than in my perception.
Pardon me for my ignorance
Bless me to bloom in this lifetime.

Acceptance

Time speeding up
When joy spreads in the air
Spending time with family
Is a love affair like no other
All the worries and anxieties
Get washed up with a wave of love
Acceptance like no other
That is what I find here.

Dreamy day

Cherry blossoms in the air
With laughter soaking in
Green grass and soft summer breeze
Make a dreamy day
To be happy again.

Melody

Right from birth
we come with a code
Each of us has our own.
We came here to live our reality
To follow the rules of our hearts.
So don't get swayed by blowing winds.
Just stay in touch with the melody within.

Do you remember?

Do you remember
The girl who was left behind?
Who gave her whole heart
Only to be stranded on the roadside.

Do you remember
Her sweet little smile?
Whose world revolved around you
Only to be broken with insincere words.

Do you remember
Leaving her humiliated?
For fights, she fought to stay by your side
Only to be left behind.

Do you remember
How she was your safe haven?
When the weather got cold and things got tough
Only to be left behind in the middle of a storm.

When you do remember,
For the sunshine, she was in your life
With a breath of spring air lighting up your sky.
A bitter truth hits your heart,
"You lost it all forever. Never will a miracle fall
into your lap again."

Partners in Crime

Related by Blood
Connected as a whole.
Younger than me,
Two little bright flowers.

One shines like the sun
Other like the moon.
One brightens the day,
Other soothes the night.

Three musketeers
Always living their best life.
On our adventures,
Making our own rules.

Love for each other
Binds us together.
Wishing the best in the world,
For one another.

On my darkest nights
They shined their light
Wiped my tears
And heard my sorrowful pain.

My wish to the shooting star,
Has been for them,
To make all their dreams come true.
And let joy overflow in their life.

One a troublemaker
One a peace bringer
And the other is a good-hearted genius
Makes up the trope of this lifetime,
Perfect partners in crime.

Ode to my Father

He remembers them all
All that is a fog for me.
My first laugh,
My first tears.
The first time I stood and fell flat on the ground.

He carried me on his shoulders,
Showing me the world.
Keeping me warm,
Protecting me from the cold.

Taught me math when I struggled,
Took me out when it got too much.
Listened to my unspoken words
And brought everything to life before I uttered a
word.

"You are unique,"
He always said.

Never let me bad talk myself.
My loudest cheerleader, hiding in the shadows.

I have always been a free spirit.
Flying like a kite
But without him holding on to the rope,
I never would have flown high.

He fought for me,
When no one would.
Stood in front of me
Against the whole world.
Like Lord Shiva, he took the poison,
Saving me only nectar.
My biggest blessing
Is being born as his daughter.

My Superhero.
My Inspiration,
He is my lighthouse
Always guiding me back home.

My first confidant.
My very best friend.
I am the luckiest daughter,
To have the greatest father in the whole world.

Ode to my Mother

To the graceful goddess of my life,
One who doesn't realize her own light.
Undermines her gifts.
Sacrifices for everyone else.

My best friend who doesn't need words to
understand,
She gets ill,
When I fall sick.
She knows in her heart everything that I feel.

The embodiment of selflessness
One I always aspire to be.
She is a beautiful flower
A rare blue that attracts envious eyes
And I became her protector to shield her from
their poisonous vines.

Her love knows no bounds,
Her scoldings were a language of concern.
Everything she does
Is for my happiness.

Everytime I ask "What makes you happy?"
She smiles with her ever patience,
"Your happiness is my happiness."
My eyes burn with unshed tears at her answer.

How can one be so kind and gentle?
While taking all the thorns on herself?
Right from when I was a helpless baby to a
selfish teenager,
She bore the burden of it all.
And even through it all, she just wants me to be
happy?

Sometimes I cannot comprehend her heart
Even as she fights her demons
She spreads joy around.
Even as people look down on her,
Based on their flawed standards.
She doesn't let their evil dampen her goodness.

She seems to me like Mother Earth herself.
Although we humans step on her and trample
down.
She still gives us food and keeps us warm.

Her compassion is unbridled,
And a force to be reckoned with.

She is a reminder that,
Power doesn't just mean ruling the world.
But power can also be in silent nurturing.
One which cannot be seen but felt.
Without which the world cannot function.
A force that binds life together but never expects
anything in return.

My Mother is more than I deserve.
A foolish daughter who hurt her way too many
times.
But I thank the god to have given me,
"The greatest mother one could ever ask for."